GROWING INFORMAL CITIES PROJECT

CALIBRATING INFORMAL CROSS-BORDER TRADE IN SOUTHERN AFRICA

SALLY PEBERDY, JONATHAN CRUSH, DANIEL TEVERA,
EUGENE CAMPBELL, INES RAIMUNDO, MAXTON TSOKA,
NOMSA ZINDELA, GODFREY TAWODZERA, NDEYAPO NICKANOR,
CHILESHE MULENGA, THUSO GREEN AND NTOMBI MSIBI

MIGRATION POLICY SERIES NO. 69

SERIES EDITOR:
PROF. JONATHAN CRUSH

SOUTHERN AFRICAN MIGRATION PROGRAMME (SAMP)
INTERNATIONAL MIGRATION RESEARCH CENTRE (IMRC)
2015

Editorial Note

In 2007-2008, SAMP planned and implemented a major regional survey of cross-border trade in Southern Africa as part of a larger project on migration, development and poverty reduction. A series of individual country reports were produced by the project. For this Growing Informal Cities Report, the individual country datasets were combined into a single regional data set. This unique dataset provides important insights into the nature of informal cross-border trade and the character of informal traders across the Southern African Development Community (SADC) region. It also provides important background for two studies conducted in Mozambique and Zimbabwe in 2014, which will be discussed in forthcoming SAMP publications. The original survey was funded by DFID-UK and the data analysis and report writing by the IDRC.

The Growing Informal Cities Project, funded by the IDRC, is a partnership between SAMP, the International Migration Research Centre (IMRC), the African Centre for Cities (ACC) at the University of Cape Town, the Gauteng City-Region Observatory and Eduardo Mondlane University.

© Southern African Migration Programme (SAMP) 2015
ISBN 978-1-920596-13-2
First published 2015
Production by Bronwen Dachs Müller, Cape Town

Printed by Megadigital, Cape Town

CONTENTS

LIST OF TABLES

EXECUTIVE SUMMARY

Informal cross-border trade (ICBT) is a significant feature of regional trade and international mobility in Southern Africa. The exact number of participants and economic importance of this trade is unknown because no official statistics are collected. Despite its obvious presence at every border post throughout the SADC region, ICBT remains largely invisible to policy-makers. Indeed, in government circles it is more often associated with smuggling, tax evasion and illegality than with innovation, enterprise and job creation. On the research side, there is a growing body of case study evidence that ICBT plays a critical role in poverty alleviation, food security and household livelihoods in Southern Africa. But its overall character and significance is unknown. With this in mind, SAMP initiated a project to examine cross-border regional trade at a selection of important border posts throughout the region. This research led to a number of country reports that provided rich insights into ICBT in particular countries. This report combines the data collected by each of the country teams and analyses the data set as a whole.

The first issue addressed in the report is whether ICBT traders are a homogenous group. The research shows that this is far from being the case and that more attention needs to be paid to different types of traders and trading activity. Second, the report examines the activities of cross-border traders including the types of goods traded, the sources of those goods and where they are sold. While the majority of traders purchase goods from formal outlets in their countries of destination, most of these goods enter the informal economy on their return home. Third, the report examines financial transactions at the borders showing that most traders pay extremely small amounts of duty, which hardly justifies the effort of collecting it. On the other hand, only a small minority collect the VAT they are owed when they leave the country of purchase. Finally, the report itemizes the problems and challenges faced by informal traders when crossing borders.

In total, the SAMP survey covered 20 land border posts connecting 11 Southern African countries using a threefold methodology. First, all people crossing through the selected border posts were monitored over a 10-day period and the number of ICBT traders counted. Second, the interactions of traders with customs officials were observed and the types, value and volumes of goods declared and duties paid were recorded. Third, a sample of traders was interviewed using an origin and destination (O&D) survey. During the course of the exercise, more than 205,000 people, including 85,000 traders, were counted passing through these border posts. The transactions of over 5,500 traders with customs officials were monitored and over 4,500 traders were interviewed.

The study demonstrates that informal cross-border is a complex phenomenon and not uniform across the region, or even through border posts of the same country. However, the overall volume of trade, duties paid and VAT foregone, as well as the types of goods and where they are produced, indicate that this sector of regional trade should be given much greater attention and support by governments of the region as well as regional organizations such as the Common Market for Eastern and Southern Africa (COMESA), SADC and the Southern African Customs Union (SACU). The major findings at the regional level were as follows:

- Demographically, women comprise a significant proportion of traders and constitute the majority of traders crossing through nearly half of the border posts surveyed, including one of the busiest at Beit Bridge between South Africa and Zimbabwe. At the same time, an unexpectedly large number of men were also involved in ICBT. Malawi and Zambia had significantly more male than female traders, for example.
- Most ICBT is bilateral in character; that is, traders tend to operate between their home country and one other country. Trading into a third country is comparatively rare. At the same time, the vast majority of traders crossing into a country with goods to sell are citizens of that country. ICBT by traders of other nationalities is uncommon.
- Although South Africa is a major source of goods purchased by traders, the absence of South African informal traders was very noticeable. The reasons why South Africans do not participate in ICBT requires further exploration but it stands in marked contrast to formal sector regional trade where South African companies predominate. ICBT is a neglected market opportunity for small-scale South African entrepreneurs and the obstacles to their participation need to be better understood.
- The majority of traders travelled frequently to other countries for short visits (sometimes for less than a day) to buy goods to sell in their home country, or to sell goods that they had bought for that purpose in their home country. Only 13% of respondents bought and sold goods while travelling (two-way trading).
- Frequency of travel also varied both within and between countries, with traders in the Namibian (42%) and Zambian (25%) surveys being most likely to travel every day. Others travel at least once a week (Mozambique, 67%; Zambia, 34%) Some travel less frequently, but at least once a month. Very few stay more than a month in another country.
- The types of goods carried by informal cross-border traders vary widely, but at most borders the trade was dominated by food, especially groceries and fresh produce. Again, there was considerable variability at different borders. New clothes, household and electrical goods comprised a significant proportion of the stock of some cross-border traders. Other goods identified in the survey included second-hand clothing, petrol, alcohol, car parts and construction materials.
- Traders mostly source their goods from the formal sector of destination

countries. A small proportion obtain their goods from informal markets in other countries. Many traders acted as wholesale importers of goods, selling the goods they carried across borders to vendors in informal markets. Others sold from their own stalls in informal markets, door to door, or to networks of family, friends and other individuals. A small proportion sold to retailers and restaurants in the formal sector.

- The value of goods carried by traders indicates the complexity and diversity of this sector. A significant cohort of traders appeared to be survivalists as many said they carried less than ZAR500 worth of goods. However, at least some of these traders travel frequently with low-value loads, rather than infrequently with high-value loads. Most traders travelled with loads in the range of ZAR1,001-5,000. A small cohort of traders travelled with loads worth more than ZAR15,000.

- Informal traders make a relatively significant contribution to duties collected at border posts. During the 10-day survey period at the 20 border posts, ZAR3,750,000 was collected from 1,780 traders. Duties collected varied between and within border posts. In some surveys the value of duties paid per trader was less than ZAR50. Interestingly, duties were being incorrectly collected at some borders between Southern African Customs Union countries (for example, between Botswana and Swaziland and South Africa). Traders said they were willing to pay duties, but wanted amounts reduced and the process to be more transparent.

- Although most traders buy their goods in the formal sector, few claim VAT when leaving the country of purchase. Many did not know they could do this while others said that the systems are too complex and time consuming. Traders who do not claim VAT back make an unintended contribution to the fiscus of the country where they buy their goods.

- Responses to questions about treatment from officials at the borders were generally positive but varied between and within border posts. Larger and busier posts generally received less favourable reviews.

The scope and scale of informal cross-border trade across the SADC suggests that it makes a significant contribution to regional trade and the retail economies of the region and is consistent with the stated aims of both the SADC and COMESA to promote intra-regional trade. Small-scale cross-border trade could, if promoted and supported, provide a route to the development of pro-poor trade policies that could have a direct impact at the household level. If trade policies for the region are to be successful, the activities of these entrepreneurs need to be included in planning processes. ICBT comprises a significant component of regional economic activity for most countries in Southern Africa. It is highly visible at border posts throughout the region. Only amongst policy-makers and governments does it remain largely invisible.

INTRODUCTION

Informal cross-border trade (ICBT) is a significant feature of regional trade flows and cross-border movements in Southern Africa.[1] However, moves to liberalize trade and promote development through trade have largely focused on large-scale formal sector trade and not cross-border trade undertaken by small-scale informal entrepreneurs. Indeed, ICBT is more often associated in official thinking with smuggling, tax evasion and illegality. COMESA, for example, defines ICBT as "unrecorded trade" which "characteristically involves bypassing border posts, concealment of goods, under-reporting, false classification, under-invoicing and other similar tricks."[2] ICBT supposedly "deprives authorities of much needed statistics, as well as revenues."[3] In addition to evading taxes or fees imposed by governments, "traders also try to avoid administrative formalities in areas such as health, agriculture, security and immigration."[4] Other organizations, such as the World Bank, take a more positive stance. The Bank has identified a series of official obstacles (both legal and illegal) to freer informal trade and proposed a Charter for Cross-Border Traders to protect their rights.[5] Despite their different attitudes towards ICBT, both COMESA and the World Bank agree that it should be formalized, regulated and brought under government control.

There is a growing body of research that shows that ICBT plays a critical role in poverty alleviation, food security and household livelihoods in Southern Africa. These studies can be divided into three main types. First, aggregate informal flows of agricultural products across borders have been monitored at various border posts for more than a decade.[6] A USAID-funded project regularly tracks the informal food trade in maize, rice and beans at over 20 border posts across the Southern African region.[7] However, only one of these monitoring sites – Beit Bridge on the Zimbabwe-South African border – captures flows out of South Africa, which is a surprising omission given South Africa's role as a major maize exporter to neighbouring countries.

A second research cluster consists of small-scale case studies focused on informal traders themselves, their profiles, activities and challenges, and their important role in poverty alleviation at the household level.[8] A sub-set of this literature on the local impacts of ICBT characterizes it as a form of "informal entrepreneurship" and focuses on the innovative income-generating and other business strategies of traders.[9]

Third, there have been attempts to combine these methodological approaches by monitoring aggregate flows of food and in-depth interviews with individual traders at border posts. In 2008, for example, a UNIFEM project interviewed 457 traders at three Zimbabwe border posts and 250 traders at three Swaziland border posts, but the results of this study have yet to be published.[10] Another project conducted by researchers at the University of Botswana interviewed 520 informal cross-border traders at four border posts between Botswana and Namibia, South Africa, Zambia and Zimbabwe and provided important insights into the profile of cross-border trade with Botswana.[11] SAMP's 2008 regional project monitored the activities of ICBT traders as they passed through 20 land border posts connecting 11 Southern African countries. This project led to a series of individual country studies which provided rich information on ICBT at the national level and analyses of destination country policy responses to the phenomenon.[12]

This report utilises the SAMP ICBT regional data set to provide an analysis of the nature of informal cross-border trade across the SADC. The first issue addressed is whether ICBT traders can be treated as a homogenous group. The research shows that there is considerable heterogeneity within ICBT and that more attention needs to be paid to different types of traders and trading activity. Second, the report examines the activities of cross-border traders including the types of goods traded, the sources of those goods and where they are sold. While the majority of traders purchase goods from formal outlets in their countries of destination, most of these goods enter the informal economy on their return home. Third, the report examines financial transactions at the borders showing that most traders pay extremely small amounts of duty, which hardly justifies the effort of collecting it. On the other hand, only a small minority collect the VAT they are owed when they leave the country of purchase. Finally, the report discusses the problems and obstacles faced by informal traders when crossing borders and how these might be addressed.

METHODOLOGY

The research for this report was undertaken by SAMP partners in eight countries at 20 border posts over a 10-day period encompassing trade between 11 SADC countries (Table 1). During the course of the survey, over 205,000 people, including 85,000 traders, were counted. The transactions of over 5,500 traders with customs officials were monitored and over 4,500 traders were interviewed. Prior to starting the research, a workshop was held with all partners to agree on a common methodology, to design the research instruments and to make a preliminary selection of border posts. The common methodology involved the development and use of three standardized research instruments for use at each border post: a counter form, a border monitors form and an origin and destination (O&D) survey.

Table 1: Border Posts Monitored		
Country	Border posts monitored	Countries of border post
Botswana	Ramokwebana Kazungula Tlokweng	Botswana/Zimbabwe Botswana/Zambia Botswana/South Africa
Lesotho	Maseru Bridge	Lesotho/South Africa
Malawi	Songwe Mwanza Dedza	Malawi/Tanzania Malawi/Mozambique Malawi/Mozambique
Mozambique	Lebombo Namaacha	Mozambique/South Africa Mozambique/Swaziland
Namibia	Oshikango Wenela	Namibia/Angola Namibia/Zambia
Swaziland	Oshoek Lavumisa	Swaziland/South Africa Swaziland/South Africa
Zambia	Livingstone Nakonde Chililabombwe	Zambia/Zimbabwe Zambia/Tanzania Zambia/DRC
Zimbabwe	Beit Bridge Chirundu Nyamapanda Mutare	Zimbabwe/South Africa Zimbabwe/Zambia Zimbabwe/Mozambique Zimbabwe/Mozambique

COUNTING

The counter form was a simple instrument that recorded the number and sex of people crossing through the border and whether these people were traders or non-traders. Counters were placed in the area between national border posts, i.e. in the "no-man's land" of the border. The primary purpose was to determine the importance of trade traffic relative to other types of border crossing as well as the sex of traders and non-traders. Several challenges to accurate enumeration were encountered. First, at borders where traffic was heavy or dominated by public transport such as buses it was difficult to count every person travelling through the border post and determine if they were traders. This led to under-counting at Beit Bridge (Zimbabwe-South Africa) and Maseru Bridge (Lesotho-South Africa). At some border posts, the project was supplied with figures by border officials themselves. Second, at border posts where large numbers of people use six-month concession passes and local passports or border permits, it was difficult to identify traders because people move quickly through the post. And third, when people were travelling in cars and buses, it was not always possible to determine whether they were traders or travelling for other reasons. In sum, these challenges meant that the number of traders passing through some borders may well have been under-counted.

BORDER MONITORING

Border monitors were stationed with customs officials on the entry side of the border of the country of survey. The purpose of the border monitoring was to record what duties were paid by traders, as well as the type, volume and value of goods on which they paid duties. The monitors recorded information on sex, nationality, type of goods declared, volume and value of goods declared, and duties paid. The border monitoring exercise was undertaken relatively successfully at all of the border posts as it was possible to determine what goods people were carrying and what duties they were paying. However, the process did have several limitations. First, of necessity, monitors were placed with the customs officials. This may have disrupted normal duty collection procedures as officials could have been more punctilious knowing that they were being observed. On the other hand, this may also have discouraged the soliciting or acceptance of bribes or other favours to avoid paying duty. Second, the sheer numbers of people passing through some border posts meant that not every trader could be monitored, and not every person or trader passing through a border encounters customs officials. Finally, with the exception of three border posts (the two in Malawi and Lavumisa in Swaziland), it was not possible to assess the contribution of duties paid by informal traders to the total amount of duties collected. However, at all posts it was possible to assess the duties paid by informal traders.

ORIGIN AND DESTINATION SURVEY

An origin and destination (O&D) survey was administered to a sample of informal traders at each border post. Participants in the O&D survey were either interviewed while queueing to pass through the border or as they left the border. Some teams found that it was not possible to interview people in queues (especially where these were short or fast-moving). The survey recorded information on the sex of the trader, the origin and destination of the journey, the purpose of journey, the type of goods carried in both directions, the value of goods being carried, the type of transport used, the type of immigration permit held, whether or not they claimed VAT, where they obtained information about customs duties payable, the time usually taken to clear the border post, where delays occur at the border post, their opinion of their treatment at the border post, and their suggestions for improved service.

The O&D survey was undertaken successfully at all border posts. However, it was not possible to draw a fully random sample of traders passing through the border posts. It was also not possible to interview traders at exactly the same part in the process of crossing borders since there are differences in the way each border post operates. Interviewers had to rely on the veracity of respondents when they described what goods they were carrying and their value as it was not possible to ask them to unpack their luggage for inspection. Because the purpose of the study was to monitor small-scale cross-border trade passing through official border posts, no attempt was made to ascertain the extent to which traders may avoid border posts altogether and/or carry their goods across borders using alternative and irregular border crossing points.[13] For example, the Tobacco Institute of Southern Africa estimates that nearly a third of the cigarettes (or 8 billion sticks) sold in South Africa in 2013 were "buttlegged" into the country, mainly from Zimbabwe. However, various researchers have challenged such figures, arguing that the actual figure is much lower and that there is no evidence of a substantial increase in cigarette smuggling.[14]

The research assistants recorded trade flows and interviewed traders as they entered their home country. The main exception was Namibia where traders were recorded and interviewed as they were leaving the country for Angola and Zambia. However, the O&D survey did ask traders questions about their business activities when they travelled into Namibia. In the Zambian survey, people moving in both directions were counted. In Swaziland, the counting activity ran into problems from officials especially at Lavumisa. As a result, only border monitoring and O&D survey data was collected.

Both SADC and COMESA gave their support to the research programme. In each country, the support and permission of relevant government departments was obtained by the country team. In all countries this necessitated the support of government departments whose remits included immigration and customs and excise. In some countries, departments suggested changes to the original selection of border posts. Key informant interviews were undertaken with government officials of relevant government departments in each country, including departments of customs and excise/revenue authority, departments of home affairs/interior/immigration and border police services. Interviews were also undertaken with officials stationed at the border posts under study as well as with traders and, where available, traders' associations.

The count of travellers crossing the surveyed border posts shows that traders constitute a significant proportion of traffic at the majority of posts. Table 2 shows that, with the exception of the border posts of Botswana and Namibia, traders comprised at least 30% of people crossing the border. In Mozambique, traders comprised over 50% of border traffic counted. The border posts of Namaacha (73%), Beit Bridge (50%), Lebombo (50%) and Nakonde (46%) had the largest proportion of traders amongst border crossers. The Botswana and Namibian border posts had the least.

Table 3 shows how many interviews were undertaken in each country with each survey instrument, as well as the number of people who were counted crossing the borders.

Table 2: Traders as a Proportion of Total Border Traffic

Country of survey	Border post of survey	Total counted	No. of traders	Traders as % of border crossers
Botswana	Tlokweng	4,223	377	8.9
	Kazangula	2,299	315	13.7
	Ramokwebana	4,131	358	8.6
	Total	10,653	1,050	9.8
Lesotho	Maseru Bridge	1,922	660	34.3
	Total	1,922	660	34.3
Malawi	Songwe	3,549	n/a	n/a
	Mwanza	9,758	n/a	n/a
	Dedza	1,835	n/a	n/a
	Total	15,142	6,492	42.8
Mozambique	Lebombo	33,948	16,795	49.5
	Namaacha	6,878	4,998	72.6
	Total	40,826	21,793	53.4
Namibia	Oshikango	9,949	1,149	11.5
	Wenela	4,327	452	10.4
	Total	14,276	1,601	11.2
Zambia	Chililabombwe	8,649	3,376	39.0
	Nakonde	74,949	34,659	46.2
	Livingstone	19,428	6,789	34.9
	Total	103,026	44,824	43.5
Zimbabwe	Beit Bridge	16,575	8,299	50.1
	Mutare	1,165	365	31.3
	Chirundu	1,647	523	31.8
	Nyamapanda	1,283	225	17.5
	Total	20,667	9,412	45.5

Table 3: Number of Traders Participating in Surveys by Country

Country of survey	Total counted	Traders counted	Border monitors survey	O&D survey respondents
Botswana	10,643	1,048	781	681
Lesotho	1,922	660	201	67
Malawi	15,142	6,492	302	328
Mozambique	40,826	21,793	500	501
Namibia	14,276	1,601	807	675
Swaziland	n/a	n/a	790	471
Zambia	103,026	44,824	766	643
Zimbabwe	20,667	9,412	1,438	1,170
Total Survey	206,502	85,830	5,585	4,536

A PROFILE OF ICBT ENTREPRENEURS

Conventional wisdom suggests that small-scale informal cross-border trade is dominated by women.[15] This study found that the picture is more complex with the proportion of female cross-border entrepreneurs varying between different SADC countries and at different border posts. Women were in the majority at half of the border posts surveyed and made up 55% of the overall number counted (Table 4). However, men were in the majority at the border posts into Zambia (78%), Malawi (68%), Namibia (65%) and Lesotho (52%). The proportion of male entrepreneurs at individual border posts ranged from a low of 10% at Kazangula (between Botswana and Zambia) to a high of 86% at Nakonde border post between Zambia and Tanzania. With regard to female entrepreneurs, the low and high figures were reversed (90% at Kazungula and 10% at Nakonde).

Table 4: Sex of Traders by Border Post and Country of Survey			
Country of survey	Border post with:	Male traders (%)	Female traders (%)
Botswana	South Africa	52	48
	Zambia	10	90
	Zimbabwe	42	58
Lesotho	South Africa	52	48
Malawi	Tanzania	64	36
	Mozambique (Mwanza)	72	28
	Mozambique (Dedza)	77	23
Mozambique	South Africa	29	71
	Swaziland	29	71
Namibia	Angola	61	39
	Zambia	74	26
Zambia	Zimbabwe	20	80
	Tanzania	86	14
	DRC	65	35
Zimbabwe	South Africa	46	54
	Zambia	33	67
	Mozambique (Mutare)	36	64
	Mozambique (Nyamapanda)	46	54

The survey found a strong correlation between the nationality of the traders and participation in informal trade in particular countries. In the survey of traders entering Mozambique, for example, 99% were Mozambicans (Table 5). The vast majority entering Lesotho, Swaziland and Zimbabwe surveys were also nationals of those countries (84% in each case). In the case of traders entering Botswana, 61% were Zimbabweans, 21% were

Zambians and only 17% were Botswana nationals. In the survey of traders leaving Namibia, 60% were Angolans and 35% were Zambians, while only 4% were Namibians. In general, the survey found low rates of participation in ICBT by South Africans and Namibians (less than 3% of the traders counted overall). These countries tend to be buying and selling destinations for traders from other countries rather than a source of informal entrepreneurs. The lack of participation by South Africans in cross-border entrepreneurship is particularly striking. South Africans certainly participate in the informal economy of their own country but very few seem to have the resources, inclination or ingenuity to extend their operations beyond their borders. This is in marked contrast to the South African formal sector where large companies are aggressively expanding into other African countries.

In the survey as a whole, the major country of origin of cross-border entrepreneurs was Zimbabwe (29% of all traders), followed by Zambia (19%), Mozambique (14%), Angola (10%), Swaziland (9%) and Malawi (8%). Breaking this down further, 84% of the entrepreneurs entering Zimbabwe were Zimbabweans as were 61% of those entering Botswana. In addition, 29% of those entering Zambia and 15% entering Lesotho were Zimbabweans. On the border with Mozambique, 84% of the traders entering Zimbabwe were Zimbabwean while only 6% were Mozambican. These findings confirm that most cross-border trade in SADC is bilateral in character but that cross-border entrepreneurs from Zimbabwe ply their trade with all of that country's neighbours as well as other countries further afield.

Table 5: Nationality of Traders by Country of Survey (% of traders)

Country of nationality	Country of survey								
	Botswana	Lesotho	Malawi	Mozam-bique	Namibia	Swaziland	Zambia	Zimbabwe	Total
Angola					60.0			0.1	10.0
Botswana	17.0								3.0
DRC					0.1		29.0		5.0
Lesotho	0.4	84.0							1.0
Malawi			94.0					2.0	8.0
Mozambique				99.0		4.0		6.0	14.0
Namibia					4.0		0.3		1.0
South Africa	0.2	1.0	0.3			11.0		3.0	2.0
Swaziland				0.4		83.0		0.3	9.0
Tanzania	0.4		3.0				0.3		0.4
Zambia	21.0		0.3		35.0		57.0	5.0	19.0
Zimbabwe	61.0	15.0	2.0		2.0		29.0	84.0	29.0
Other	0.3		0.6	0.4		2.0			0.3

The traders were asked what kind of immigration permits they were using to cross the border. The majority said they did not need a permit, although this varied considerably from less than 1% in the case of Mozambique to 93% in the case of Malawi (Table 6). The Malawian figure is so high probably because the question was seen as referring to entry to Malawi. A similar interpretation may have been placed on the question in the Botswana survey (where 68% said they did not need a permit). The majority of traders overall entered other countries on short-term visitors permits. The numbers were particularly high in the case of Swazi traders going to South Africa (90%), Mozambicans going to South Africa and Swaziland (80%) and Zimbabweans leaving the country (50%). Traders entering Lesotho (82%) and Zambia (47%) and leaving Namibia (80%) appear to make most use of local permits (also known as border passes or six-month concessions), which generally allow multiple entries and quick passage through borders. Most traders reported that the type of permit they held did not restrict them from carrying on their business. Traders travelling to another country to buy goods generally do not violate the terms of their permits. However, those who sell in another country may well be breaking the conditions of their visitors and local permits.

Table 6: Type of Permits used by Traders (% of traders)					
Country of survey	No permit required	Visitors permit	Local permit	Permanent resident	Other
Botswana	68	4	5	20	2
Lesotho	6	10	82	0	7
Malawi	93	5	0	0	2
Mozambique	1	80	1	0	18
Namibia	4	13	79	1	3
Swaziland	0	90	2	0	8
Zambia	22	19	47	1	10
Zimbabwe	16	51	27	3	2

PURPOSE OF TRADE

Nearly 90% of the ICBT entrepreneurs captured in the survey were "one-way traders"; that is, they bought goods in one country and sold them in another (Table 7). Over half (53%) said the purpose of their journey was to buy goods in another country for their business at home and a third said their purpose was to take goods from their home country to sell in another country. Only 13% were "two-way traders" who bought and sold goods in both their country of origin and destination. However, the picture is more complex than these aggregate figures suggest with considerable variation between countries and border posts. Over 80% of the traders entering Lesotho, Mozambique and Swaziland, for example, were bringing back goods for their businesses at home. More than half of those entering Malawi (60%) and Zambia (58%) were in a similar position. However, there were differences between border posts. Almost all traders entering Zambia through Nakonde had been to shop for goods in Tanzania. Between Zambia and Zimbabwe and Zambia and the Democratic Republic of the Congo (DRC) there was more of a balance between traders who were bringing and those taking goods to sell.

In sharp contrast, the largest proportion of Zimbabweans (48%) were two-way traders. Only 27% had left without anything and were returning with goods to sell in Zimbabwe. An even smaller number (21%) only exported goods from Zimbabwe. The preponderance of two-way traders was replicated at all of the Zimbabwean border posts except Livingstone (with only 5% being two-way traders). At Mutare, the figure was two thirds, at Nyamapanda 48%, at Beit Bridge 42% and at Chirundu just over a third. Given the dire economic situation in Zimbabwe at the time of the survey, two-way trading was clearly a business strategy to make profit in both countries. However, the prevalence of two-way trading is still surprising since it is not immediately clear what goods Zimbabweans were taking out of the country to sell (see below). The other anomalous finding concerns Botswana where only a quarter were bringing goods back to sell; a clear reflection of the availability of most goods within the country and its economic strength. Informal export of goods from Botswana to other countries was far more common with two thirds of the entrepreneurs involved in this form of trade.

Table 7: Main Purpose of Journey (% of traders)				
	One-way traders		Two-way traders	Other
Country of survey	Bringing back goods to sell	Taking goods to sell		
Botswana	25	66	7	2
Lesotho	81	19	-	0
Malawi	60	37	3	0.0
Mozambique	81	1	12	6
Namibia	54	44	1	0
Swaziland	88	8	1	2
Zambia	58	37	5	1
Zimbabwe	27	21	48	4
Total Survey	53	32	13	2

TYPES AND VALUES OF TRADED GOODS

The types of goods carried by ICBT entrepreneurs across borders proved to be many and varied (Table 8). Foodstuffs, including fresh produce and groceries, constituted the most significant category of goods transported across borders. A total of 27% of the traders were carrying foodstuffs (8% groceries and 27% fresh produce). Groceries were most likely to be carried by those entering Mozambique and Zimbabwe (70% of traders in both cases). This was particularly evident at the borders between South Africa and Mozambique, Zimbabwe and Mozambique and Zimbabwe and South Africa. Almost 30% of all traders entering Zambia and over half (56%) of traders coming from Zimbabwe were also carrying groceries, as were half of those travelling between Namibia and Angola and Zambia. By contrast, very little fresh produce was being carried into a number of countries including Zimbabwe (2% of traders), Swaziland (7%) and Malawi (7%).

The most important corridors for fresh produce were between Botswana and Zambia (37% of traders), the DRC and Zambia (32%), South Africa and Lesotho (31%), South Africa and Botswana (30%), South Africa and Mozambique (21%), and Swaziland and Mozambique (also 21%). Meat, fish and eggs were carried by only 1% of traders. Mozambique was the major exception with almost two thirds of traders carrying one or more of these items. As many as three quarters crossing into Mozambique at the Lebombo border post with South Africa were in possession of foodstuffs. This may be explained by the close proximity of farming and shopping areas in South Africa and Swaziland to the main destination of Maputo, making problems of spoilage less likely.

Given that 45% of traders overall had ferried goods out of their home country to sell in another country, it is important to get some sense of what they were carrying and selling. What stands out, once again, is the importance of trade in foodstuffs (Table 9). The proportion of traders who reported carrying groceries out of their home country ranged from a low of 14% in the case of Malawi to a high of 40% in the case of Mozambique. The export of fresh produce was less important but there were significant flows at some border posts, including between Mozambique and Zimbabwe.

CLOTHING

Trade in second-hand clothing has been identified as a significant component of ICBT in several Southern African countries.[16] There is a large market in second-hand clothes in the informal economy in Maputo, but only 1% of the traders were bringing in used clothing from South Africa or Swaziland (Table 8). This suggests that informal cross-border entrepreneurs are not involved in this business and that the clothes are sourced elsewhere

Table 8: Type of Goods Imported to Home Country (% of traders)

Country of survey and border post	Groceries	Fresh fruit and vegetables	Meat/fish/eggs	Electrical goods	Furniture	House-hold goods	New clothes/shoes	Second-hand clothes/shoes	Handi-crafts/curios	Other
Botswana	8	27	1	1	1	16	16	3	10	21
South Africa	45	30	-	1	-	3	49	3	-	10
Zambia	19	37	4	1	-	7	8	7	3	13
Zimbabwe	4	20	0.2	1	1	22	9	2	15	27
Lesotho	10	31	1	-	-	6	13	4	10	24
Malawi	18	7	0.3	20	1	23	38	-	0.3	24
Mozambique	70	21	61	6	1	4	12	1	-	9
South Africa	76	21	75	1	-	0.4	6	-	-	6
Swaziland	64	21	47	10	2	8	18	1	-	12
Namibia	56	16	6	3	1	8	3	0.1	2	19
Swaziland	4	7	0.4	3	1	19	56	9	1	10
South Africa (Oshoek)	6	17	4	9	5	22	42	1	1	17
South Africa (Lavumisa)	3	2	0.3	1	-	19	63	12	1	7
Zambia	29	14	8	4	1	8	22	16	3	16
Zimbabwe	56	3	2	-	1	3	2	2	9	-
Tanzania	14	2	2	6	1	9	52	33	1	-
DRC	20	32	17	5	0.4	11	14	14	1	-
Zimbabwe	69.5	1.6	1.5	7.7	0.6	2.9	9.8	1.9	0.1	3.1
South Africa	71.1	2.3	0.3	14.5	1.3	3.1	4.1	1.8	0	1.6
Mozambique (Mutare)	88.7	1.0	4.4	-	-	1.0	1.0	-	0.5	3.4
Zambia	36.8	1.4	1.4	3.5	-	2.8	37.5	5.6	-	4.2
Mozambique (Nyamapanda)	72.6	-	-	1.4	-	8.2	9.6	-	-	0

* Note percentages may add up to more than 100%. Multiple answers were allowed as many carried mixed loads.

Table 9: Type of Goods Exported from Home Country (% of traders)

Country of survey	Groceries	Fresh fruit and vegetables	Meat/fish/eggs	Electrical goods	Furniture	House-hold goods	New clothes/shoes	Old clothes/shoes	Crafts/curios	Other
Botswana	31	6		10		10	31	6	<0.1	10
Malawi	14	5	14	5	9		27		14	18
Mozambique	40	33					4	6	2	-
Swaziland	15	8	4	4			8		4	15
Zambia	22	27	22			12	19	6		5
Zimbabwe	32	13	4	2	2	9	12	0.5	19	8

and transported into Mozambique by other means. In the region as a whole, only 3% of traders were carrying second-hand clothing across borders for resale, although 16% of those entering Zambia were involved in the trade. More important were new clothing and shoes (carried by 16% of the traders), although their importance varied from country to country and border to border. At the South Africa-Botswana border, for example, 49% of traders entering Botswana were carrying new clothes and shoes. Some 56% of traders entering Swaziland were also trading in new clothing and shoes. The other significant trade in these goods was into Malawi, with 38% of traders involved. On the other hand, only 10% of traders entering Zimbabwe, and 12% entering Mozambique, carried new clothing and shoes for resale.

None of the other countries, besides Zambia, were important markets for second-hand clothing. Around 6% of traders said they had taken second-hand clothing out of Botswana, Mozambique and Zambia to sell in other countries. Again, as with imports, exports of new clothing were more important (Table 9). Close to 30% of traders entering Botswana and Malawi said that they had left these countries with new clothes and shoes to sell. Zimbabwe was the most important destination for these traders. Around a third of traders at the Zimbabwe borders with Zambia and Mozambique also said that they had exported new clothes and shoes from Zimbabwe to these countries.

HOUSEHOLD AND OTHER GOODS

Cross-border traders throughout the region were carrying electrical and other household goods but not much furniture, which is bulky and difficult and expensive to transport. Traders travelling to Malawi were most likely to be carrying household goods into the country (23%), followed by Swaziland (19%) and Botswana (16%) (Table 8). While South Africa is clearly the most important source of household goods for resale in other countries, it is not the only one; for example, of the traders returning to Zimbabwe from Mozambique 21% said that they had exported household goods on their outward journey (Table 9).

The survey uncovered a large range of other goods being carried by smaller numbers of traders. These varied from country to country but included *chitenges* and *capulanas* (pieces of cloth worn by women in Southern and Eastern Africa) and other types of fabric, liquor/alcohol, car parts, cars, hardware, construction materials and sundry goods. The Namibian survey revealed a substantial trade in petrol to Angola and Zambia, but often carried in the petrol tanks of vehicles rather than in jerry cans. Petrol is also transported to Zimbabwe from Francistown in Botswana in a similar manner. Once in the destination country, the petrol is siphoned and sold. This trade goes unrecorded so its extent and importance is impossible to determine.

HANDICRAFTS

The import of handicrafts and curios to the study countries was quite limited (since these countries tend to be sources rather than markets). In total, 10% of the traders were carrying handicrafts and curios, primarily into Lesotho and Botswana (Table 8). There is probably a market for Zimbabwean handicrafts amongst tourists visiting these two countries, which could explain their importation by small-scale entrepreneurs. More significant was the export of handicrafts, particularly from Zimbabwe. A total of 19% of the traders entering Zimbabwe said they had exported handicrafts from the country (Table 9). The most important site was Beit Bridge between Zimbabwe and South Africa where as many as 42% of traders said that they had exported handicrafts to South Africa.

VALUE OF GOODS

The majority of traders entering Botswana, Lesotho, Mozambique, Swaziland and Zambia were carrying goods worth less than ZAR1,000 (Table 10). A major exception to the general rule of low-value trading was at the South African border with Zimbabwe, where 57% of traders were carrying goods valued at between ZAR1,000 and ZAR5,000. Nearly 30% of Zimbabwean traders at all border posts were carrying goods valued at over ZAR2,000. Another exception to the rule was at the Zambia-Tanzania border where three quarters of the traders were carrying goods valued at between ZAR2,000 and ZAR10,000 and another 16% were carrying goods worth over ZAR10,000. At other Zambian border posts, low-value trading was more the norm. Higher-value trading was also evident at the Malawian border posts where less than 20% of traders carried goods worth ZAR1,000 or less. A further 55% had goods worth between ZAR1,001 and ZAR5,000 and 26% had goods worth more than ZAR5,000.

Table 10: Value of Goods Carried by Traders (% of traders)							
Country of survey	ZAR1-500	ZAR501-1,000	ZAR1,001-2,000	ZAR2,001-5,000	ZAR5,001-10,000	ZAR10,001-15,000	Over ZAR15,000
Botswana	80.3	12.2	4.8	1.3	0.2	0.0	0.0
Lesotho	62.7	16.4	13.4	4.5	1.5	1.5	0.0
Malawi	7.5	11.6	23.5	31.6	11.9	7.5	6.4
Mozambique	30.4	28.5	21.3	14.9	1.8	0.5	2.2
Swaziland	7.9	54.0	19.6	6.0	4.5	0.0	8.1
Zambia	44.0	10.3	6.6	16.0	16.3	4.0	2.8
Zimbabwe	23.6	11.9	36.7	20.2	6.1	1.6	0.0

The diversity and range of value of the goods carried by traders suggests that ICBT includes a broad spectrum of entrepreneurs, from small-scale survivalists to relatively large-scale traders. It suggests that there could be possibilities for bringing those at the high end of the spectrum into the formal sector, while raising questions about the costs of negotiating border regulations for those at the lower end of the spectrum.

CONDUCTING BUSINESS

Traders used a variety of transport modes to travel to and from border posts. The choice of mode is influenced by the distances travelled, the location of border towns, the volume of goods being transported and the charges levied by the transport carrier. The most common form of transport used by traders to cross borders was buses and minibus taxis (Table 11). At every border post, with the exception of the Namibia and Angola border, more than half of the traders travelled to and from the border using this form of transport. Given the sheer volume of traders on the roads, this means that they make a significant contribution to the private transport industry. Traders travelling by car were likely to be have been missed by interviewers, so the proportion travelling by car may be underestimated.

Informal cross-border traders exhibit a complex variety of travel patterns, even through a single border post (Table 12). Traders using border posts where border towns were in relatively close proximity travelled frequently. Some crossed the border more than once a day on a regular basis (for instance at Livingstone, Kasumbalesa, Mutare and Namaacha). Others made their journey a few times a week. Those using border posts where distances to buying and selling areas were longer tended to travel once a week, bi-monthly or once a month. Malawians were most likely to travel bi-monthly or monthly. This was also true for Zimbabweans. A smaller proportion of traders travelled only twice a year or less.

Not surprisingly, the length of stay in countries of destination tended to be short (Table 13). Patterns of stay reflected patterns of travel: as travel became more frequent, length of stay tended to decrease. The majority of traders at most border posts crossed for a day or less. Of the rest, most were likely to spend less than a week in another country. Other research indicates that traders are reluctant to spend too long in another country, especially if they are there to shop and not to sell as well.[17] This is because they worry about their security and that of their goods and money. Furthermore, accommodation can be expensive and/or uncomfortable. Traders from Botswana, Malawi and Zimbabwe tended to stay away longer than those from other countries, probably because they had further to travel and were also engaged in buying and selling. In the case of Botswana, 47% stayed abroad for a week or longer. The equivalent figures for Malawi and Zimbabwe were 35% and 26% respectively.

Table 11: Mode of Transport Used by Traders To and From Borders (% of traders)

Country of survey	Direction of travel	Bus/taxi	Car/van	Truck	Foot	Bike	Train
Botswana	To border	78	8	0	14	0	0
	From border	91	8	0	1	0	0
Lesotho	To border	64	36	0	0	0	0
	From border	64	36	0	0	0	0
Malawi	To border	96	1	2	0	0	0
	From border	90	3	6	0	0	0
Mozam-bique	To border	73	8	1	10	0	7
	From border	76	5	1	17	0	1
From Namibia	To border	32	6	1	46	14	0
	From border	39	6	1	40	14	0
Swaziland	To border	71	21	6	2	0	0
	From border	50	39	5	6	0	0
Zambia	To border	68	1	0	27	1	3
	From border	79	1	1	18	1	1
Zimbabwe	To border	76	12	8	4	1	0
	From border	78	11	8	3	1	0

Table 12: Frequency of Travel to Another Country for Trade (% of traders)

Country of survey	Once a day or more	Few times a week	Once a week	Twice a month	Once a month	Twice a year or less
Botswana	3	12	8	13	53	9
Lesotho	4	22	6	18	45	1
Malawi	2	2	6	37	33	20
Mozambique	10	38	29	8	13	1
From Namibia	41	31	17	3	5	3
Swaziland	2	6	8	18	55	11
Zambia	24	25	9	14	19	9
Zimbabwe	10	11	8	18	36	17

Table 13: Length of Stay in Destination Country (% of traders)

Country of survey	One day or less	2-3 days	4-7 days	1-2 weeks	3-4 weeks	1 month or more
Botswana	27	16	10	41	3	3
Lesotho	61	22	6	4	4	1
Malawi	17	24	24	22	7	6
Mozambique	66	21	10	2	1	0
From Namibia	93	3	0	1	1	1
Swaziland	31	63	2	3	1	0
Zambia	77	11	7	2	2	1
Zimbabwe	25	32	13	16	6	4

An analysis of the purchasing behaviour of informal cross-border traders shows that they contribute significantly to the formal sector wholesale and retail economies of the countries where they buy their goods. The majority sourced their goods from formal sector wholesalers and retailers. Wholesalers were particularly important sources of goods for traders leaving Namibia (79%), and traders from Malawi (64%) and Zambia (53%) (Table 14). Retailers (mainly supermarkets) were more important than wholesalers for traders from Zimbabwe (60%), Mozambique (55%), Lesotho (42%) and Swaziland (34%). Traders also contributed to the informal economy in destination countries, particularly those from Zambia (40%), Swaziland (38%) and Botswana (24%). Although most bought foodstuffs and agricultural products from formal and informal sector retailers and wholesalers, some traders from Botswana, Lesotho and Mozambique sourced their goods directly from commercial and smallholder farms.

Table 14: Type of Outlet Where Goods are Bought (% of traders)						
Country of survey	Wholesaler	Retailer	Informal market	Commercial farm	Smallholder farm	Other
Botswana	18	12	24	4	16	24
Lesotho	16	42	3	25	1	9
Malawi	64	41	16	1	1	7
Mozambique	39	55	4	12	0.4	2
From Namibia	79	23	3	0.3	0.1	3
Swaziland	18	34	38	3	1	5
Zambia	53	16	40	0	2	3
Zimbabwe	24	60	14	1	1	1
* Note totals may add up to more than 100% as respondents could provide multiple answers.						

While traders make a significant contribution to the formal sector of countries where they purchase their goods, they contribute primarily to the informal sector when selling (Table 15). The proportion of traders who sold to formal shops, retailers and restaurants was very low in all countries, although it was marginally more important in Malawi (15% of traders) and Zambia (14% of traders). Some cross-border traders, especially in Malawi (at 57%), owned the shops where they sold the goods they imported into the country. It is unclear if these shops were in the formal or informal sector. Larger proportions of traders in the other countries tended to sell from their own stalls in informal markets or sold to others who operate in those markets. In general, informal markets were the major outlet for the sale of imported goods in countries such as Mozambique (75% of traders), Zambia (54%), Lesotho (45%) and Zimbabwe (38%). The only countries where informal markets were relatively unimportant were Malawi and Swaziland. The other significant means of disposing of goods in some countries (especially Botswana and Lesotho) was through door-to-door sales. Others sold through networks of friends, family members and others. This was the most important way of selling goods in Swaziland (44%), Zimbabwe (40%) and Zambia (39%). Door-to-door selling and networking were of little importance in Mozambique.

Table 15: Outlets for Goods (% of traders)							
Country of survey	Own shop	Own stall in informal market	Other sellers in informal markets	Door to door	Friends/ family/ networks	Retailers/ shops/res-taurants	Other
Botswana	3	20	12	30	25	3	5
Lesotho	1	18	27	31	22	0	0
Malawi	57	8	12	16	17	15	10
Mozambique	8	55	20	9	6	7	9
From Namibia	23	39	31	14	9	1	2
Swaziland	10	15	8	19	44	4	3
Zambia	5	24	30	6	39	14	1
Zimbabwe	4	8	31	7	40	8	1

FINANCIAL TRANSACTIONS AT BORDERS

During the 10-day survey period at the 20 border posts, more than ZAR3,750,000 was collected from 1,780 traders – an average duty payment of ZAR2,106 per trader (Table 16). However, as the researchers were not able to monitor all interactions between traders and customs officials, the amount of duty collected was undoubtedly higher. Extrapolating from this data, an estimated ZAR135 million was collected in 2008 from small-scale traders at these 20 border posts alone. In total, only 37% of the traders paid customs duties on their goods although there was considerable variation by border post and country. No traders returning to Lesotho, and only 3% of those entering Zimbabwe, paid customs duties, for example.

At the other end of the spectrum, virtually all traders entering Malawi were charged customs duties, as were 78% of those entering Botswana and 75% of those entering Zambia. The demands for customs duties also varied considerably between border posts, often between the same two countries. For example, 36% of traders entering Swaziland from South Africa through Oshoek paid duties compared to only 6% at Lavumisa, the other border post between the two countries. Such variability, especially between border posts of the same country, suggests that the regulations and levying of customs duties are very unevenly applied. In general, the small amounts collected from most traders call into question the cost-effectiveness of the whole exercise.

Table 16: Duties Paid by Country and Border Post				
Country of survey and destination countries	No. of traders paying duty	Percentage of traders paying duty	Total duties paid (South African rands)	Average duty per trader (South African rands)
Botswana				
South Africa	152	94	15,724	103.45
Zambia	58	28	17,886	308.38
Zimbabwe	403	97	29,721	73.75
Total	613	78	63,331	103.31
Lesotho				
South Africa	0	0	0	0
Total	0	0	0	0
Malawi				
Tanzania	157	100	140,582	895.43
Mozambique (Mwanza)	49	96	33,228	678.12
Mozambique (Dedza)	94	100	45,816	487.40
Total	300	99	219,627	732.09
Mozambique				
South Africa	29	12	-	-
Swaziland	5	2	-	-
Total	34	7	-	-
Swaziland				
South Africa (Oshoek)	192	36	76,565	398.78
South Africa (Lavumisa)	16	6	6,242	390.12
Total	208	26	82,807	398.11
Zambia				
Zimbabwe	207	99	31,648	152.89
Tanzania	370	99	101,697	274.86
DRC	9	4	34,00	3.78
Total	586	75	133,379	227.61
Zimbabwe				
South Africa	2	0	570	285.00
Zambia	2	1	428	219.00
Mozambique (Mutare)	29	7	1,514	52.21
Mozambique (Nyamapanda)	6	7	1,470	245.00
Total	39	3	3,954	101.38
TOTAL	1,780	37	3,754,154	2,109.18

Nearly 3,000 traders did not pay any duties. These traders were generally carrying goods valued at below the personal allowance and/or tariff rate. None of the researchers observed bribes being offered or taken when they were monitoring the interactions between customs officials and traders.

They did, however, note the various methods used by traders to avoid paying duty. For example, some traders paid people to carry some of their goods across the border for them so the individual loads fell under the personal allowance limit. At some border posts, traders hired people to take goods around rather than through the border post and met them on the other side.

Tariff regimes are certainly complex with different tariff rates for different goods. If traders are not informed about the amount of duties payable on goods, their lack of knowledge could be exploited by unscrupulous customs officials. There certainly proved to be significant differences in levels of knowledge about the customs requirements (Table 17). Traders entering Mozambique were the best informed with the overwhelming majority (92%) saying they had information about the duties they were required to pay. Traders entering Swaziland, Botswana and Zambia were the least informed with half or less saying they had the requisite information. In all of the countries, over half of traders said they got their information from customs although it is not clear how this information was conveyed. Other traders were the second most important source of information. Traders' associations were of negligible importance. Other sources cited included the media, town clerks and clearing agents.

Table 17: Knowledge About Duty Payable at Customs (% of traders)				
Country of survey	Yes	No	Sometimes	No answer
Botswana	45	38	11	6
Lesotho	46	54		
Malawi	74	23	3	
Mozambique	92	7	1	
Namibia/Angola	58	41	1	
Swaziland	41	54	2	3
Zambia	50	45	4	
Zimbabwe	64	31	5	

Traders who carry goods with receipts that include valued-added tax (VAT) are eligible to claim the VAT when leaving the country of purchase. The various methods for claiming VAT are often complex and time consuming. Refunds may be made out in cheques or deposits to credit cards and are rarely paid in cash. The vast majority of traders did not claim VAT from the countries where they bought their goods (Table 18). Those entering Malawi (30%) and Mozambique (33%) were most likely to have claimed VAT. Almost all traders entering Zambia (94%) said they did not claim VAT and over three quarters of those interviewed entering Botswana, Swaziland and Zimbabwe also said they did not claim. There was some variation between border posts. Traders using some of the larger border posts, e.g., Beit Bridge (39%) and Oshoek (33%) were most likely to claim VAT.

Table 18: Claims for VAT by Traders (%)				
Country of survey	Yes	No	Sometimes	No answer
Botswana	8.2	76.8	0.9	14.1
Lesotho	6.0	94.0	0.0	0.0
Malawi	30.2	66.5	2.1	1.2
Mozambique	32.5	63.9	3.0	0.6
Swaziland	17.7	77.1	3.6	1.5
Zambia	2.0	94.4	0.3	3.3
Zimbabwe	19.3	77.1	3.6	0.0

Although most informal traders are viewed as operating outside the regulatory and tax framework, they do contribute to the national tax base of the country of purchase when they fail to claim VAT that may be owed to them. When asked why they did not claim VAT, most traders said they did not know they were eligible or how to claim, that it took too long and that they were unable to cash cheques (Table 19). Amongst the other reasons given were that the process was too complicated to make it worthwhile.

Table 19: Reasons Why Traders Did Not Claim VAT (%)						
Country of survey	Don't know how to claim	Takes too long	Cannot cash cheque	Other	Not applicable	No answer
Botswana	47.7	1.5	0.5	4.8	38.6	6.9
Lesotho	98.4	0.0	0.0	1.6	0.0	0.0
Malawi	46.9	10.4	0.9	34.6	1.4	5.7
Mozambique	35.7	8.0	1.4	34.1	20.8	0.0
Swaziland	60.3	15.3	0.0	16.9	7.5	0.0
Zambia	94.7	1.4	0.3	0.5	0.0	3.1
Zimbabwe	50.3	17.5	6.2	0.0	22.9	0.0

TREATMENT AT THE BORDER

Four out of five traders said they encountered major problems when crossing borders. The problems that were identified fell into three categories: customs-related, immigration-related and border post operations (Table 20). Over a quarter of the traders said duties were too high, and a fifth said that sometimes the duties they had to pay were more than the cost of the goods they were carrying. Other problems cited included variable duties and arbitrary setting of charges by customs officials. Around 5% of the traders said the confiscation of goods or detention of goods by customs officials was a problem. Some alleged that customs officials then sold their goods for personal gain. Traders at some border posts complained about restrictions placed on the import of specific goods into the DRC (maize), Angola (alcohol) and Zambia (sugar and beer).

Table 20: Major Problems Encountered by Traders at Borders		
Problem	No.	%
Customs-related		
Duties paid are too high	741	27
Tariffs/duties always fluctuate/Customs set own charges	184	7
Unwarranted confiscation/detention of goods	135	5
Restrictions on import of goods (type and volume)	95	3
Lack of information on customs procedure	16	1
VAT claim cumbersome/issuing of cheques is problem	13	0.5
Immigration-related		
Lack of permits/high cost of permits	76	3
Days allowed in recipient country are too few	28	1
Border post operations		
Long queues/congestion/delays	701	25
Too much corruption	189	7
Staff unfriendly/rude/impatient/unnecessary questioning	164	6
Transport problems/poor road networks/transport prices high	137	5
Physical harassment/beating/violation of human rights	64	2
Checkpoints cause delays	52	2
Bureaucracy/service/computer breakdown causes delays	43	2
Security poor/border unsafe because of criminals	28	1
Poor infrastructure/lack of toilets/bad toilets	19	1
Total	2,782	100
Note: More than one answer permitted. Percentages refer only to those who said there were problems.		

Immigration formalities seemed to pose less of a problem for traders. Because a significant proportion of interviewees are not required to hold permits to travel to countries where they do business, this is perhaps not surprising. Those who did complain mentioned the lack and cost of permits and the length of stay allowed. Although most traders at most border posts were able to complete formalities in less than half an hour, delays and congestion were identified as a major problem by over a quarter of traders. Corruption was also identified as a problem by 7% of traders. Unfriendly, rude, impatient officials were identified as a problem by 6% of respondents. A further 2% (64 traders) complained of physical harassment and beating. Insecurity and crime were seen as problematic by a small number (2%). Transport was also raised as an issue by some with references to poor roads, the high cost of transport and problems with transporting their goods.

The traders had several suggestions for border improvements. In terms of customs, 30% said duties should be reduced but only 1% suggested that they should be scrapped altogether. This suggests that traders accept that they may have to pay duties, but it is the amounts demanded that are a problem for them. A few suggested that small-scale traders should pay duties at a lower rate than large-scale traders and some that duties for small traders should be charged at a fixed rate. Others indicated that pamphlets and notice boards could be introduced to inform traders about customs procedures and tariff rates as well as their rights and obligations.

Few had suggestions for improving the immigration regime, which suggests an acceptance of the status quo. But service quality figured significantly in suggestions for improvement. Nearly a third wanted to see expedited and improved services through the employment of greater numbers of border personnel. In the same vein, a smaller number wanted to see better customer care and an end to harassment. Also related to efficiency at the border post, some suggested separate queues for traders, non-traders and locals. Others recommended separate traffic queues for trucks/lorries and light vehicles. Other recommendations for improving facilities at border posts were that foreign exchange facilities should be introduced so they could change their money and that enquiry desks be established.

Table 21: Suggestions to Improve Service at Border Posts		
Suggestion	N	%
Customs-related		
Reduce customs duties	635	30
End corruption/punish corrupt officials	83	4
Apply duties for small traders at lower rates than large	47	2
Pamphlets, notices to inform on customs procedures/clarify rights and obligations	40	2
Charge fixed amount	35	2
Training of customs officials for better assessment of goods	7	0.3
Stop filling of forms and search of luggage	7	0.3
Immigration-related		
Increase number of days allowed in recipient country	19	1
Free entry and exit between countries	19	1
Border post operations		
Employ more staff to expedite service/improve service	638	30
Better customer care/stop harassment	127	6
Improve road network/transport services	86	4
Upgrade computer system	52	2
Improve security	31	1
Improve infrastructure to increase efficiency (including toilets)	26	1
Make separate queues for traders/non-traders/locals	15	1
Total	2,144	100

CONCLUSION

This study, the largest of its kind ever undertaken in SADC, shows that small-scale cross-border traders comprise a significant proportion of traffic through border posts throughout the region. With the exception of the border posts of Botswana and Namibia and the Nyamapanda border between Mozambique and Zimbabwe, traders comprised over 30% of people going through these border posts during the period of the SAMP survey. They constituted half of border crossers counted at Beit Bridge between South Africa and Zimbabwe and almost three quarters at Namaacha between Swaziland and Mozambique.

The majority of traders travelled frequently for short visits (often less than a day) to other countries to buy goods for re-sale in their home countries. Very few stayed more than a few days in another country. Only 13% of the respondents both imported and exported goods when they travelled. This group of "two-way" traders was dominated by Zimbabweans (almost half of the Zimbabwean traders fell into this category). The type of goods carried by small-scale cross-border traders varied widely between border posts and trading corridors, but was dominated by food items including groceries, fresh fruits and vegetables as well as meat, fish and eggs. New clothes, household and electrical goods also comprised a significant proportion of the stock of small-scale cross-border traders.

The variety in the values of the loads of goods carried by traders indicates the complexity and diversity of this sector of trade. A significant cohort of traders appeared to be survivalists. Many carried under ZAR500 worth of goods when crossing. However, when combined with the frequency of travel and length of stay, it seems that some traders prefer to travel frequently with low-value loads, rather than infrequently with high-value loads. Most traders travelled with loads valued in the range of ZAR1,000-ZAR5,000 although a small cohort of traders had loads worth more than ZAR15,000. Although they are often labelled as "informal", and therefore operating outside regulatory frameworks, the traders made a significant contribution to the duties collected at border posts. While traders were willing to pay duties, they wanted the rules to be transparent and less arbitrary and amounts to be reduced. Tariff regimes in the region are certainly complex and only half of the traders said they had information about what customs duties were payable. Although most traders bought their goods in the formal sector where VAT is payable, few claimed VAT on a regular basis because the process is time-consuming and complicated. They therefore make a contribution to the fiscus of the country in which they buy their goods.

The patterns of trade undertaken by these small entrepreneurs are complex. They travel to a wide variety of destinations, including major cities, small towns and even villages. Cities and towns comprise the majority of destinations, while border towns did not figure as prominently as expected as destinations. ICBT therefore forms a complex web of entrepreneurial interactions which extends across the region encompassing rural and urban areas. ICBT also straddles and links the formal and informal economies of the region. The scale and scope of trade uncovered suggests that it makes a significant contribution to regional trade and the retail economies of the region and is consistent with the stated aims of both the SADC and COMESA to promote intra-regional trade. The participation of small-scale traders suggests that ICBT could, if promoted further, provide a route to the development of pro-poor trade policies that could have a direct impact at the household level. The significant participation of women in this sector of regional trade suggests that it also provides opportunities for the economic empowerment of women.

If trade policies for the region are to be successful, the activities of these male and female entrepreneurs need to be included in planning processes. The range of values of duties collected and traders' comments on the collection of duties raise questions about tariff regimes in the region. When devising plans to improve efficiency at land border posts the activities of these traders need to be taken into account; and, as regular users of border posts, their opinions could be of considerable value. Overall, the study shows that small-scale cross-border trade comprises a significant component of regional economic activity for most countries in Southern Africa. It is highly visible at border posts throughout the region and to the officials that staff these posts. Only to policy-makers and governments does ICBT remain largely invisible.

ENDNOTES

1   C. Lesser and E. Moisé-Leeman, "Informal Cross-Border Trade and Trade Facilitation Reform in Sub-Saharan Africa" OECD Trade Policy Papers No. 59, Paris, 2009; I. Chirisa, "The Role of the Informal Sector in African Regional Integration: Scope and Limits" *Insight on Africa* 6(2014): 2131-44.

2   N. Njiwa, "Tackling Informal Cross-Border Trade in Southern Africa" *Bridges Africa* 2(2013): 9-11.

3   Ibid.

4   Ibid.

5   P. Brenton, N. Dihel, M. Hoppe and C. Soprano, "Improving Behaviour at Borders to Promote Trade Formalization: The Charter for Cross Border Traders" World Bank Policy Note No. 41, Washington DC, 2014.

6   C. Ackello-Ogutu, "Methodologies for Estimating Informal Cross-Border Trade in Eastern and Southern Africa" Technical Paper No. 29, USAID Africa Bureau, Washington DC, 1996; I. Minde and T. Nakhumwa, "Informal Cross-Border Trade between Malawi and her Neighbouring Countries" Agricultural Policy Research Unit, University of Malawi, 1997; I. Minde and T. Nakhumwa, "Unrecorded Cross-Border Trade between Malawi and Neighbouring Countries" Technical Paper No. 90, USAID Africa Bureau, Washington DC, 1998; J. Macamo, "Estimates of Unrecorded Cross-Border Trade between Mozambique and her Neighbors: Implications for Food Security" USAID Africa Bureau, Washington DC, 1998; J. Mwaniki, "The Impact of Informal Cross Border Trade on Regional Integration in SADC and its Implications on Wealth Creation" IRED, Geneva, 2003; W. Burke and R. Myers, "Spatial Equilibrium and Price Transmission between Southern African Maize Markets Connected by Informal Trade" *Food Policy* 49(2014): 59-70.

7   FEWSNET and WFP, "Informal Cross-Border Food Trade in Southern Africa" Issue No. 78, Famine Early Warning Systems Network and World Food Program, Johannesburg, 2012.

8   V. Muzvidziwa, "Cross-Border Trade: A Strategy for Climbing out of Poverty in Masvingo, Zimbabwe" *Zambezia* 25(1998): 29-58; J. Parsley, "Free Markets, Free Women? Changing Constructions of Citizenship and Gender Relations among Cross-Border Women Traders in Contemporary Southern Africa" MA Thesis, Wits University, Johannesburg, 1998; N. Nethengwe, "Cross-Border Dynamics in Southern Africa: A Study of Informal Cross-Border Trade between South Africa and Zimbabwe" MA Thesis, Wits University, Johannesburg, 1999; V. Muzvidziwa, "Zimbabwe's Cross-Border Women Traders: Multiple Identities and Responses to New Challenges" *Journal of Comparative African Studies* 19(2001): 67-80; V. Muzvidziwa, *Informal Cross-Border Trade among Women in the Southern Africa Development Community* (Addis Ababa: OSSREA, 2006); W. Kachere, "Informal Cross Border Trading and Poverty Reduction in the Southern African Development Community: The Case of Zimbabwe" PhD Thesis,

University of Fort Hare, 2011; C. Chivani, "Informal Cross-Border Trade: A Review of Its Impact on Household Poverty Reduction (Zimbabwe)" M.Soc.Sci. Thesis, University of Fort Hare, 2008; V. Muzvidziwa, "Cross-Border Traders: Emerging, Multiple and Shifting Identities" *Alternation*, 19(2012): 217-38; T. Jamela, "Experiences and Coping Strategies of Women Informal Cross-Border Traders in Unstable Political and Economic Conditions: The Case of Bulawayo (Zimbabwe) Traders" M.Dev. Studies Thesis, University of Johannesburg, 2013.

9   S. Peberdy, "Mobile Entrepreneurship: Informal Cross-Border Trade and Street Trade in South Africa" *Development Southern Africa* 17(2000): 201-19; S. Peberdy, "Border Crossings: Small Entrepreneurs and Informal Sector Cross Border Trade between South Africa and Mozambique" *Tjidschrift voor Economische en Sociale Geographie* 91(2000): 361-78; S. Peberdy and J. Crush, "Invisible Trade, Invisible Travellers: The Maputo Corridor Spatial Development Initiative and Informal Cross-Border Trading" *South African Geographical Journal* 83(2001): 115-23; S. Peberdy and C. Rogerson, "Transnationalism and Non-South African Entrepreneurs in South Africa's Small, Medium and Micro-Enterprise Economy" In J. Crush and D. McDonald (Eds.) *Transnationalism and New African Immigration to South Africa* (Toronto: CAAS and SAMP, 2002); P. Mazengwa, "A Business Analysis of Zimbabwean Cross Border Trading" MA Thesis, University of Natal, Durban, 2003; N. Chiliva, R. Masocha and S. Zindiye, "Challenges Facing Zimbabwean Cross Border Traders Trading in South Africa: A Review of the Literature" *Chinese Business Review* 12(2011): 564-70; N. Ama, K. Mangadi and H. Ama, "Exploring the Challenges Facing Women Entrepreneurs in Informal Cross-Border Trade in Botswana" *Gender in Management: An International Journal* 29(2014).

10   T. Ndiaye, "Sharing the Findings of the Baseline Studies on Women in Informal Cross Border Trade in Africa" Presentation at ECA/ATPC Inception Workshop on Mainstreaming Gender into Trade Policy, Addis Ababa, 2009.

11   N. Ama, O. Mangadi, K. Okurut and H. Ama, "Profitability of the Informal Cross-Border Trade: A Case Study of Four Selected Borders of Botswana" *African Journal of Business Management* 7(2013): 4221-32; N. Ama, K. Mangadi and H. Ama, "Characterization of Informal Crossborder Traders Across Selected Botswana Borders" *International Journal of Management and Marketing Research* 7(2014): 85-102.

12   E. Campbell and Z. Mokomane, "Informal Cross-Border Traders in Botswana" SAMP Report, University of Botswana, Gaborone, 2008; T. Green, "Small Scale Cross Border Trade Study: Lesotho Report" SAMP Report, Sechaba Consultants, Maseru, 2008; C. Mulenga, "Small-Scale Cross Border Trade between Zambia, Democratic Republic of the Congo, Tanzania and Zimbabwe" SAMP Report, Institute of Economic and Social Research, University of Zambia, Lusaka, 2008; N. Nickanor, M. Conteh and M. Eiseb, "Unpacking Huge Quantities into Smaller Units: Small-Scale Cross Border Trade Between Namibia and her Northern Neighbours" SAMP Report, University of Namibia, Windhoek,

2008; I. Raimundo and B. Cau, "Border Monitoring of Cross Border Trade: Mozambique" SAMP Report, Eduardo Mondlane University, Maputo, 2008; D. Tevera and G. Tawodzera, "Cross Border Trade: The Case of Beitbridge, Forbes, Chirundu and Nyamapanda Border Posts" SAMP Report, University of Zimbabwe, Harare, 2008; M. Tsoka, "Cross Border Trade Study: Malawi" SAMP Report, Centre for Social Research, University of Malawi, Lilongwe; N. Zindela, "Informal Cross Border Trade in Swaziland" SAMP Report, University of Swaziland, Kwaluseni, 2008.

13 See, for example, N. Pophiwa, "Smuggling on the Zimbabwe-Mozambique Border" In J. Crush and D. Tevera, (Eds.), *Zimbabwe's Exodus* (Ottawa and Cape Town: IDRC and SAMP, 2010), pp. 291-306; M. Bolt, "Waged Entrepreneurs, Policed Informality: Work, the Regulation of Space and the Economy of the Zimbabwean-South African Border" *Africa* 82(2012): 111-30; S. Yikona, B. Slot, M. Geller, B. Hansen and F. el Kadiri, *Ill-Gotten Money and the Economy: Experiences from Malawi and Namibia* (Washington DC: World Bank, 2012) O. Akinboade, M. Mokwena and W. Grobler, "Factors Determining International Migrants' Involvement in Illegal Trade in South Africa" *Mediterranean Journal of Social Sciences* 5(2014).

14 E. Blecher, "A Mountain or a Molehill: Is the Illicit Trade in Cigarettes Undermining Tobacco Control Policy in South Africa?" *Trends in Organized Crime* 13(2010): 299-315; C. van Walbeek, "Measuring Changes in the Illicit Cigarette Market using Government Revenue Data: the example of South Africa" *Tobacco Control* doi:10.1136/tobaccocontrol-2013-051178.

15 Chiliva et al. "Challenges Facing Zimbabwean Cross Border Traders."

16 A. Brooks, "Riches from Rags or Persistent Poverty? The Working Lives of Secondhand Clothing Vendors in Maputo, Mozambique" *Textile* 10(2010): 222-37.

17 Peberdy and Crush, "Invisible Trade, Invisible Travelers"; K. Lefko-Everett, "The Voices of Zimbabwean Migrant Women in South Africa" In Crush and Tevera, *Zimbabwe's Exodus*, pp. 269-90.

MIGRATION POLICY SERIES

1. *Covert Operations: Clandestine Migration, Temporary Work and Immigration Policy in South Africa* (1997) ISBN 1-874864-51-9

2. *Riding the Tiger: Lesotho Miners and Permanent Residence in South Africa* (1997) ISBN 1-874864-52-7

3. *International Migration, Immigrant Entrepreneurs and South Africa's Small Enterprise Economy* (1997) ISBN 1-874864-62-4

4. *Silenced by Nation Building: African Immigrants and Language Policy in the New South Africa* (1998) ISBN 1-874864-64-0

5. *Left Out in the Cold? Housing and Immigration in the New South Africa* (1998) ISBN 1-874864-68-3

6. *Trading Places: Cross-Border Traders and the South African Informal Sector* (1998) ISBN 1-874864-71-3

7. *Challenging Xenophobia: Myth and Realities about Cross-Border Migration in Southern Africa* (1998) ISBN 1-874864-70-5

8. *Sons of Mozambique: Mozambican Miners and Post-Apartheid South Africa* (1998) ISBN 1-874864-78-0

9. *Women on the Move: Gender and Cross-Border Migration to South Africa* (1998) ISBN 1-874864-82-9.

10. *Namibians on South Africa: Attitudes Towards Cross-Border Migration and Immigration Policy* (1998) ISBN 1-874864-84-5.

11. *Building Skills: Cross-Border Migrants and the South African Construction Industry* (1999) ISBN 1-874864-84-5

12. *Immigration & Education: International Students at South African Universities and Technikons* (1999) ISBN 1-874864-89-6

13. *The Lives and Times of African Immigrants in Post-Apartheid South Africa* (1999) ISBN 1-874864-91-8

14. *Still Waiting for the Barbarians: South African Attitudes to Immigrants and Immigration* (1999) ISBN 1-874864-91-8

15. *Undermining Labour: Migrancy and Sub-contracting in the South African Gold Mining Industry* (1999) ISBN 1-874864-91-8

16. *Borderline Farming: Foreign Migrants in South African Commercial Agriculture* (2000) ISBN 1-874864-97-7

17. *Writing Xenophobia: Immigration and the Press in Post-Apartheid South Africa* (2000) ISBN 1-919798-01-3

18. *Losing Our Minds: Skills Migration and the South African Brain Drain* (2000) ISBN 1-919798-03-x

19. *Botswana: Migration Perspectives and Prospects* (2000) ISBN 1-919798-04-8

20. *The Brain Gain: Skilled Migrants and Immigration Policy in Post-Apartheid South Africa* (2000) ISBN 1-919798-14-5

21. *Cross-Border Raiding and Community Conflict in the Lesotho-South African Border Zone* (2001) ISBN 1-919798-16-1

22. *Immigration, Xenophobia and Human Rights in South Africa* (2001) ISBN 1-919798-30-7

23. *Gender and the Brain Drain from South Africa* (2001) ISBN 1-919798-35-8

24. *Spaces of Vulnerability: Migration and HIV/AIDS in South Africa* (2002) ISBN 1-919798-38-2

25. *Zimbabweans Who Move: Perspectives on International Migration in Zimbabwe* (2002) ISBN 1-919798-40-4

26. *The Border Within: The Future of the Lesotho-South African International Boundary* (2002) ISBN 1-919798-41-2

27. *Mobile Namibia: Migration Trends and Attitudes* (2002) ISBN 1-919798-44-7

28. *Changing Attitudes to Immigration and Refugee Policy in Botswana* (2003) ISBN 1-919798-47-1

29. *The New Brain Drain from Zimbabwe* (2003) ISBN 1-919798-48-X

30. *Regionalizing Xenophobia? Citizen Attitudes to Immigration and Refugee Policy in Southern Africa* (2004) ISBN 1-919798-53-6

31. *Migration, Sexuality and HIV/AIDS in Rural South Africa* (2004) ISBN 1-919798-63-3

32. *Swaziland Moves: Perceptions and Patterns of Modern Migration* (2004) ISBN 1-919798-67-6

33. *HIV/AIDS and Children's Migration in Southern Africa* (2004) ISBN 1-919798-70-6

34. *Medical Leave: The Exodus of Health Professionals from Zimbabwe* (2005) ISBN 1-919798-74-9

35. *Degrees of Uncertainty: Students and the Brain Drain in Southern Africa* (2005) ISBN 1-919798-84-6

36. *Restless Minds: South African Students and the Brain Drain* (2005) ISBN 1-919798-82-X

37. *Understanding Press Coverage of Cross-Border Migration in Southern Africa since 2000* (2005) ISBN 1-919798-91-9

38. *Northern Gateway: Cross-Border Migration Between Namibia and Angola* (2005) ISBN 1-919798-92-7

39. *Early Departures: The Emigration Potential of Zimbabwean Students* (2005) ISBN 1-919798-99-4

40. *Migration and Domestic Workers: Worlds of Work, Health and Mobility in Johannesburg* (2005) ISBN 1-920118-02-0

41. *The Quality of Migration Services Delivery in South Africa* (2005) ISBN 1-920118-03-9

42. *States of Vulnerability: The Future Brain Drain of Talent to South Africa* (2006) ISBN 1-920118-07-1

43. *Migration and Development in Mozambique: Poverty, Inequality and Survival* (2006) ISBN 1-920118-10-1

44. *Migration, Remittances and Development in Southern Africa* (2006) ISBN 1-920118-15-2

45. *Medical Recruiting: The Case of South African Health Care Professionals* (2007) ISBN 1-920118-47-0

46. *Voices From the Margins: Migrant Women's Experiences in Southern Africa* (2007) ISBN 1-920118-50-0

47. *The Haemorrhage of Health Professionals From South Africa: Medical Opinions* (2007) ISBN 978-1-920118-63-1

48. *The Quality of Immigration and Citizenship Services in Namibia* (2008) ISBN 978-1-920118-67-9

49. *Gender, Migration and Remittances in Southern Africa* (2008) ISBN 978-1-920118-70-9

50. *The Perfect Storm: The Realities of Xenophobia in Contemporary South Africa* (2008) ISBN 978-1-920118-71-6

51. *Migrant Remittances and Household Survival in Zimbabwe* (2009) ISBN 978-1-920118-92-1

52. *Migration, Remittances and 'Development' in Lesotho* (2010) ISBN 978-1-920409-26-5

53. *Migration-Induced HIV and AIDS in Rural Mozambique and Swaziland* (2011) ISBN 978-1-920409-49-4

54. *Medical Xenophobia: Zimbabwean Access to Health Services in South Africa* (2011) ISBN 978-1-920409-63-0

55. *The Engagement of the Zimbabwean Medical Diaspora* (2011) ISBN 978-1-920409-64-7

56. *Right to the Classroom: Educational Barriers for Zimbabweans in South Africa* (2011) ISBN 978-1-920409-68-5

57. *Patients Without Borders: Medical Tourism and Medical Migration in Southern Africa* (2012) ISBN 978-1-920409-74-6

58. *The Disengagement of the South African Medical Diaspora* (2012) ISBN 978-1-920596-00-2

59. *The Third Wave: Mixed Migration from Zimbabwe to South Africa* (2012) ISBN 978-1-920596-01-9

60. *Linking Migration, Food Security and Development* (2012) ISBN 978-1-920596-02-6

61. *Unfriendly Neighbours: Contemporary Migration from Zimbabwe to Botswana* (2012) ISBN 978-1-920596-16-3

62. *Heading North: The Zimbabwean Diaspora in Canada* (2012) ISBN 978-1-920596-03-3

63. *Dystopia and Disengagement: Diaspora Attitudes Towards South Africa* (2012) ISBN 978-1-920596-04-0

64. *Soft Targets: Xenophobia, Public Violence and Changing Attitudes to Migrants in South Africa after May 2008* (2013) ISBN 978-1-920596-05-7

65. *Brain Drain and Regain: Migration Behaviour of South African Medical Professionals* (2014) ISBN 978-1-920596-07-1

66. *Xenophobic Violence in South Africa: Denialism, Minimalism, Realism* (2014) ISBN 978-1-920596-08-8

67. *Migrant Entrepreneurship Collective Violence and Xenophobia in South Africa* (2014) ISBN 978-1-920596-09-5

68. *Informal Migrant Entrepreneurship and Inclusive Growth in South Africa, Zimbabwe and Mozambique* (2015) ISBN 978-1-920596-10-1

www.ingramcontent.com/pod-product-compliance
Lightning Source LLC
Chambersburg PA
CBHW080556270326
41929CB00019B/3331